YOUR KNOWLEDGE H

Raja Praveen.k.n

A Trusted Cloud Computing With Cryptographic Technique

GRIN Verlag

Bibliografische Information der Deutschen Nationalbibliothek:

Die Deutsche Bibliothek verzeichnet diese Publikation in der Deutschen National-
bibliografie; detaillierte bibliografische Daten sind im Internet über http://dnb.d-
nb.de/ abrufbar.

Imprint:

Copyright © 2013 GRIN Verlag GmbH
Druck und Bindung: Books on Demand GmbH, Norderstedt Germany
ISBN: 978-3-656-50890-8

GRIN - Your knowledge has value

Der GRIN Verlag publiziert seit 1998 wissenschaftliche Arbeiten von Studenten, Hochschullehrern und anderen Akademikern als eBook und gedrucktes Buch. Die Verlagswebsite www.grin.com ist die ideale Plattform zur Veröffentlichung von Hausarbeiten, Abschlussarbeiten, wissenschaftlichen Aufsätzen, Dissertationen und Fachbüchern.

Visit us on the internet:

http://www.grin.com/

http://www.facebook.com/grincom

http://www.twitter.com/grin_com

A Trusted Cloud Computing With Cryptographic Technique

By: - Rajapaveen k.N*

2013

Table of Contents

ACKNOWLEDGEMENT

First of all, I am thankful to God almighty that made me able to complete my work successfully. I sincerely convey my thanks to my beloved Vice – chancellor & our founder, first Bishop YESHU DARBAR,   Rev. Fr. Prof.(Dr.) Rajendra B. Lal for his guidance ,support and help in each and every aspect , and I also convey my thanks to my mother and grandmother Mrs.Swarnalatha.N & M. Amulya Prema for their parental guidance

Author: Rajapraveen.k.N

Abstract

This book focuses on the security issues in Cloud Computing System; Cloud Computing is an upcoming paradigm that offers tremendous advantages in economical aspects such as reduced time to market, flexible computing capabilities and limitless computing power. To use the full potential of the cloud computing, data is transferred, processed and stored by external cloud providers. However, data owners are very skeptical to place their data outside their own control sphere. This book discusses the security controls to protect data in cloud computing environment using Cryptographic technique.

Cloud computing provide the way to share distributed resources and services that belong to different organizations. Since cloud computing share distributed resources via the network in the open environment, thus it makes security problems important for us to develop the cloud computing application. In this book, we pay attention to the security requirements in cloud computing environment. We proposed a method to build a trusted computing environment using cryptographic technique, for cloud computing system by integrating the trusted computing platform into cloud computing system. Security has become a major concern in cloud computing environment. Where the resources are shared by many. Users join and leave the cloud dynamically which leads to a serious challenge for the security of shared resources. Hence there's a need to establish trust in the cloud so that the users are ensured of their data security. We propose a model system in which cloud computing system is combined with trusted computing platform with trusted platform module. In this model, some important security services, including authentication, confidentiality, data Storage, data security and access control, are provided in cloud computing system.

Chapter – I
Introduction

Clouds computing is the collective term for a group of computing resources, distributed systems and network computing were used wildly, Cloud computing is a model for providing convenience, on-demand network access to a shared pool of computing resources like., servers, networks, applications, storage, and services) that can be provisioned and released with management effort or service provider interaction. security has become major problem in the cloud computing system. Users from various multiple environments use the distributed computing resources more efficiently. Cloud computing is concerned with the sharing and coordinated use of diverse resources in distributed organizations --- cloud, which is consisted of different organizes and systems. Cloud computing provides a facility that enable large-scale controlled sharing and interoperation among resources that are dispersedly owned and managed. Security is therefore a major element in any cloud computing infrastructure, because it is necessary to ensure that only authorized access is permitted and secure behavior is accepted. In a word, all members in the cloud and the cloud computing environment should be trusted by each other, and the members that have communication should be trusted by each other. Trust is the major concern of the consumers and provider of services. Those participate in a cloud computing environment. Because the cloud computing is composed of different local systems and includes the members from multiple environments, therefore the security in cloud is complicate. The security mechanism should provide guarantees secure enough to the user;

"A Trusted Cloud Computing with Cryptographic Technique" is a trusted computing platform which acts as a Security Solution in Cloud computing Environment. We proposed important security Characteristics for security concern. We propose a new way (Cryptographic Technique) that is conducive to improve the secure and dependable computing in cloud environment. In our design, we integrate Trusted Computing Platform (TCP), which is based on Trusted Platform Module (TPM), into the cloud computing system.

5

1.1 Product Prospective

1.1.1 Existing System

In the existing system, for the cloud computing security has many merits, but still there will be some lack of mechanism to support the trusted computing in cloud computing environment. The trusted root in cloud computing environment has not been defined clearly. The creation of protection is not secure enough for cloud computing environments. There is also lack of mechanism to register and classify the participants carefully such as tracing and monitoring. In the existing system, authentication, confidentiality and integrity are provided.

1.1.2 Proposed System

In the proposed system, we introduce a method to build a trusted computing environment for cloud computing system using Cryptographic technique as major concern, by integrating the Trusted Computing Platform (TCP) into cloud computing system. We propose a model system in which cloud computing system is combined with existing modules as basic factor to develop a new module using Cryptographic techniques to provide cloud security in more efficient way. "*A Trusted Cloud Computing with Cryptographic technique*" is a proposed security system that provides security Parameter on both aspects (USER & CLLOUD SERVICE PROVIDER)

1.2 Objectives

1. To ensure Authentication, Confidentiality, Data Security, Data Storage and Integrity in cloud computing environment using Cryptographic technique as a major concern.
2. To ensure storage of Cloud customer data will be secure and authentic.

Chapter – II

Materials and Methods

2.1 Cloud Computing System

Cloud Computing is a pool of computing resources that are provided by different venders and can be accessible by user Remote Computer without any installation of software. Cloud Computing is a technology that uses the internet and central remote servers to maintain data and applications. Cloud computing allows consumers and businesses to use applications without installation and access their personal files at any computer with internet access.

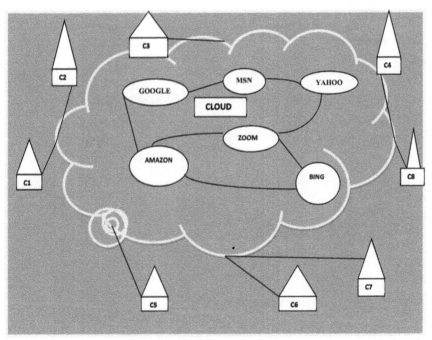

Figure 2.1: Cloud Computing System

C1,C2,C3,C4,C5,C6,C7,C8 : Cloud Customers
Amazon, Google, Msn, Bing : Cloud Providers

The above figure represents the working of cloud computing system and how a cloud computing system will works. c1,c2,c3,vc4,c5,c6,c7,c8 are the cloud users accessing the cloud computing resources from various vendors like GOOGLE, MSN, YAHOO, BING..Etc.

2.2 Architecture of Cloud Computing System

A Cloud is a type of parallel and distributed system consisting of a collection of interconnected and virtualized computers that are dynamically provisioned and presented as one or more unified computing resources based on service-level agreements established through negotiation between the service provider and consumers.

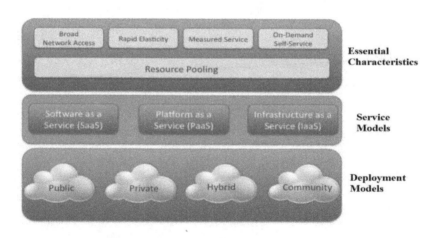

Figure 2.2: Cloud computing system Architecture

Important features of cloud computing is given below:

- Cloud Service Models
- Cloud Deployment Models
- Essential Characteristics of Cloud Computing

8

2.2.1 Cloud Service Models

Cloud Software as a Service (SaaS), Network – Hosted application

Software-as-a-Service, process by which Application Service Provider (ASP) provides different software applications over the Internet. This makes the user to get rid of installing and operating the application on own computer and also eliminates the tremendous load of software maintenance; continuing operation, safeguarding and support.

Ex: facebook, youtube

Cloud Platform as a Service (PaaS), Network – Hosted software development platform

Platform as a Service is the delivery of a computing platform that provides the service without software downloads or installation for end-users. It provides an infrastructure with a high level of integration in order to implement and test cloud applications. user does not manage the infrastructure (including network, servers, operating systems and storage), but user controls deployed applications and their configurations.

Ex of PaaS : Google App Engine

Cloud Infrastructure as a Service (IaaS), Provider Network storage

Infrastructure as a Service enhances the sharing of hardware resources for executing services using Virtualization technology. The main objective is to provide resources such as servers, network and storage. Thus, it offers basic infrastructure on-demand services and using Application Programming Interface (API) for interactions with hosts, switches, and routers, and the capability of adding new equipment in a simple and transparent manner. In general, the user does not manage the underlying hardware in the cloud

Infrastructure, but user controls the operating systems, storage and deployed applications. The service provider owns the equipment and is responsible for housing, running and maintaining it. User typically pays on a per-use basis.

Ex of IaaS: Amazon Elastic Cloud Computing (EC2)

2.2.2 Cloud Deployment Models

Public Cloud, The cloud infrastructure is made available to the general public or a large industry group and is owned by an organization selling cloud services.

Private Cloud, The cloud infrastructure is operated solely for a single organization. It may be managed by the organization or a third party, and may exist on-premises or off-premises.

Community Cloud, The cloud infrastructure is shared by several organizations and supports a specific community that has shared concerns (e.g., mission, security requirements, policy, or compliance considerations). It may be managed by the organizations or a third party and may exist on-premises or off-premises

Hybrid Cloud, The cloud infrastructure is a composition of two or more clouds (private, community, or public) that remain unique entities but are bound together by standardized or proprietary technology that enables data and application portability (e.g., cloud bursting for load-balancing between clouds).

2.2.3 Essential Characteristics of Cloud Computing

Benefits of Cloud Computing:

- Business Benefits of Cloud Computing
- Technical Benefits of Cloud Computing

2.3 Security of Cloud Computing System Architecture

The architecture was designed to encompass a wide variety of tools and technologies. It provides strong user authentication, blocks the access of unsafe endpoints and coordinates security devices across the enterprise. The Trusted Computing technology is used to improve the security of cloud computing system.

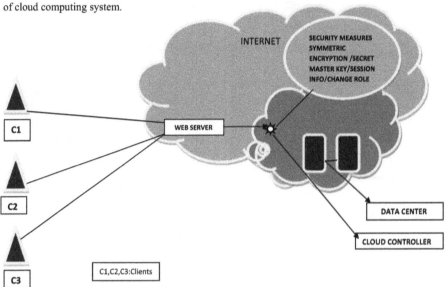

Figure: 2.3 Security of Cloud Computing System Architecture

Trusted Computing was developed and promoted by the Trusted Computing Group. The word is taken from the field of trusted systems and has a specific meaning. For security enhancement Here we generate the "Unique secret key" for each machine, that admin can make authentication for all he users. The security reasons concern to the cloud users we generate a cryptographic key called as symmetric key. By using this symmetric key cloud user security will authentic.

2.4 Trusted Cloud Computing with Cryptographic Technique

Need of Trusted Computing, problems of widely used security applications is to protect the hardware platform against attacks on its integrity or modification of the security software. Within the PC area typical incidents and attacks are well known and are endangering PCs for home banking, but also on servers within companies and some other organizations which are used for very sensible and important data, like personal, e-commerce and billing few others. In embedded systems such incidents happen. examples are illegal changes or manipulations of data in controllers within automotive systems, e.g. odometer values for increasing the car value or vehicle theft protection systems but also other embedded system which handle goods of value. Current approaches for solving this problem purely at the software level are by their very principle unpromising. As has since been amply confirmed from experience and security trends in the smart card world, a trusted and tamperproof security basis cannot be implemented using software-based solutions alone. This of course applies equally to host systems such as PC platforms as well as embedded controllers.

Trusted Computing Group, Major companies in the PC sector have therefore joined forces and worked to solve this problem with the aid of a new hardware approach and the creation of an associated industry standard. In 1999 Compaq, Hewlett-Packard, IBM, Intel and Microsoft established the Trusted Computing Platform Alliance; main aim was to create Trusted Clients. In order to make important applications like networks, communications and e-commerce more trustworthy. The emerging Trusted Computing Standard employs a secure hardware structure whose main component, the Trusted Platform Module (TPM), is specified as an LSI security chip. This Standard is largely based on recent years' experience with high-security smart cards and their applications, important parts of whose architecture and security characteristics have been consistently adopted. Similarly to the way in which we use the smart cards cryptographic mechanisms to protect sensitive and confidential personal data as well as critical processes in a security environment, these functions can also be used in the TPM to ensure not only the integrity of a platform but also to protect its user data.

Standardization: TCG, The TCG is an industry standards group with a membership of more than

80 computing companies and offers standards that span computing devices, from PCs and servers to mobile devices and peripherals. The TCG has since agreed three important specifications:

- Trusted Platform Module (TPM).
- PC Specific Implementation Specifications.
- TCG Software Stack Specifications (TSS).

These parts set out the basic prerequisites for secure components on the new secure platforms, corresponding member companies have similarly been investing considerable resources to ensure that the first implementations are available and that the first trusted motherboards with TPM or complete PC systems are ready for shipment. At the same time, however, standardization work is continuing. In a total of around 20 working groups, the next application options and interfaces are being planned and standardized.

2.4.1 Cryptographical Security Mechanisms

In this dissertation we propose *symmetric key encryption* as a major concern to provide security services mainly from user side. Uses the cryptographic key to transform the original message into an encrypted form. Decryption does the reverse; it uses a cryptographic key to transform an encrypted message back into its original (plaintext) form. A key is just a number, or a sequence of bits, which is large enough, so that it cannot be guessed or discovered in a systematic way.

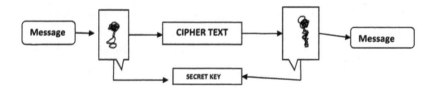

Figure 2.4 Symmetrical Cryptographic Process for Encryption - and Decryption Process

2.5 Implementation Tools

To Development of "A Trusted Cloud Computing with Cryptographic Technique" developed by using Cryptographic technique (symmetric key encryption) as a major concern to provide security parameter for both parties (Cloud user & Cloud Service Provider) to achieve this we integrating the trusted computing technology into the cloud computing system. To ensure security measures in cloud computing system, following Modules has been proposed.

Modules

Trusted computing platform is integrated into cloud computing which provides security to the cloud. This system contains the following modules to provide security for our cloud computing system.

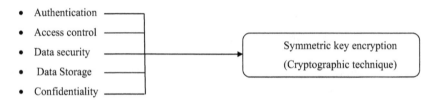

- Authentication
- Access control
- Data security
- Data Storage
- Confidentiality

Symmetric key encryption
(Cryptographic technique)

2.5.1.1 Authentication

Cloud Admin Security parameter, The Service provider (administrator) of Cloud computing System provides security for the cloud resources and cloud users. Basing the request from users, service provider can generate the unique id to the users to become cloud users. So that cloud users have an authentication to utilize cloud resources. He can trace out the users information, using Cloud history cloud Also he can interact with the cloud users through mail.

Cloud Customer Security parameter, Cloud Customer will upload the files into cloud with having security authentication properly; whenever a cloud customer uploaded a file into concern cloud

14

cryptographic symmetric key will be generated, if admin want to access the cloud user files he should get approval with users symmetric key.

2.5.1.2 Access control

Cloud users can use the cloud resources based on their access control. Cloud users may have accessibility like 'read' and 'write'. The cloud user who has read accessibility can only use the resources which are available in the cloud. And the cloud user who has write accessibility can have permissions to upload files into cloud. These cloud users can interact with cloud service provider to get change of their accessibility.

2.5.1.3 Data Security

The Service provider can provide security to the data (resources of cloud and cloud users). Symmetric key are used for encryption of data to sustain the security of data for a session. Cloud users can provide security through their private master id.

2.5.1.4 Confidentiality

Here we proposed the confidentiality module in safe and secure way for user data storage & data security in the cloud computing system can be achieved by using symmetric key.

2.5.1.5 Data Storage

The cloud customer data that has been stored in the cloud is completely secure with proper authentication. With symmetric key encryption. Using symmetric encryption the storage of date will become more secure, only authenticated users can able to access the cloud information.

2.6 Implementation Procedure for "A Trusted Cloud Computing with Cryptographic Technique"

Trusted computing technology provides certain security constrains in cloud computing environment, trusted cloud computing mainly dealing with secrets and additional functions which would normally include both dealing with secrets. However, the trusted cloud computing technology contains some functions using cryptographic technique (symmetric key) as major concern.

Cloud computing environment, with Trusted Computing Platform Data protection is a more than just a subject of maintenance in the wrong people out of places they shouldn't be and not having valuable records disappear. Data protection is a driven by a host of new legal requirements that protect the customer privacy. Different entities can appeal to join the cloud computing environment. The initial step is to verify their identities to the cloud computing system administration to get approval for entering into Cloud computing environment.

Because cloud computing should involve a large amount of entities, such as users and resources from different sources, the authentication is important and complicated, trusted computing technology contain a private *Unique key* for which can provide authenticated security services from admin side. If admin want to access any data that related to cloud user, Admin should be very securely accessed with getting approval permission from Concern user with specific Symmetric key, cloud computing service should present which role it will give the permission, when the cloud computing service notifies itself to the cloud -computing environment. So the user will able to know whether he could make access to that cloud computing service before his action. The Symmetric encryption is another major mechanism in our design. This function lets data be encrypted using Symmetric key in such a way that it can be decrypted only by a certain machine, and only if that machine is in a certain configuration. As a result, data encrypted for a particular configuration cannot be decrypted when the machine is in a different configuration... The distributed environment, we can use this function to transmit data to remote machine and this data can be decrypted when the remote machine has certain configuration. When user wan to upload any file in to cloud it will generate symmetric for every file, if cloud customer uploaded 10 files into the Cloud environment it will generate 10 symmetric keys it means 1:1 ratio. By this

16

type of technique confidentiality can be archived and data storage & data security will be more authentic.

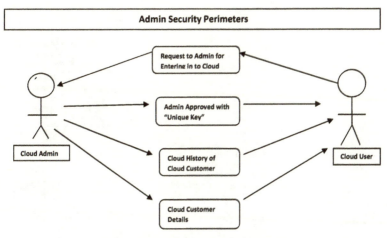

Figure 2.5: Admin Security Parameters

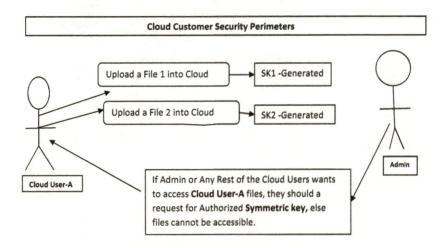

Figure 2.6: Cloud Customer Security Parameters

17

2.6.1 Class Diagram

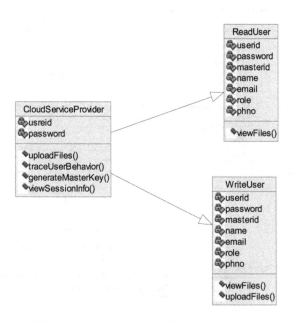

Figure 2.7: Class Diagram

18

2.6.2 Sequence Diagram

Cloud Service Provider

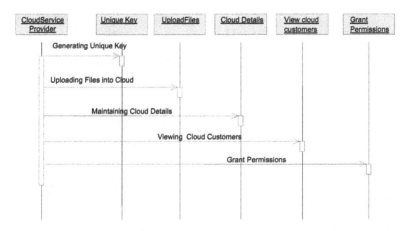

Read User

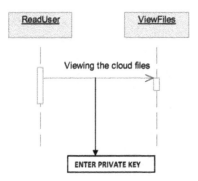

Write User

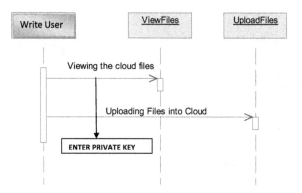

Figure 2.8 Sequential Diagram

Chapter - III

Result and Discussion

3.1 Performance parameters

After developing *"A Trusted Cloud Computing with Cryptographic Technique"* the trusted computing mechanism can provide a way that can help to establish a security environment. This model of trusted computing is designed to provide the privacy and trust, in the personal platform.

The model *"A Trusted Cloud Computing with Cryptographic Technique"*, Proposed new security parameters in the cloud computing system using Cryptographic technique as major concern.

Parameters of Current System

- Current Existing system according to Zhidong Shen, international school of software, wuhan university, China.

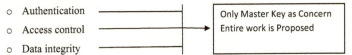

- o Authentication
- o Access control
- o Data integrity

Only Master Key as Concern
Entire work is Proposed

Parameters of Proposed System

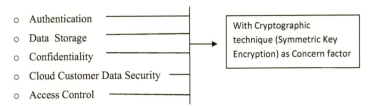

- o Authentication
- o Data Storage
- o Confidentiality
- o Cloud Customer Data Security
- o Access Control

With Cryptographic technique (Symmetric Key Encryption) as Concern factor

In the proposed system we use Existing concept as a basic point of preference and taken few modules into consideration for better enhancement of security system in cloud computing environment.

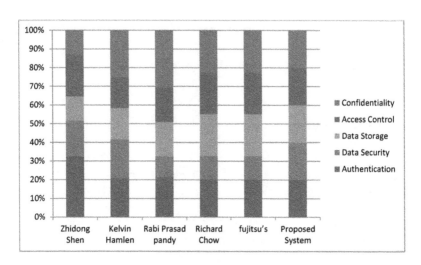

Chart: 3.1 Comparative Charts for the Existing Features

- Adding Additional features like cryptographic technique into existing system. the security in cloud computing System will be more secure(Authentic, Confidential, data integrity and Security of user data)

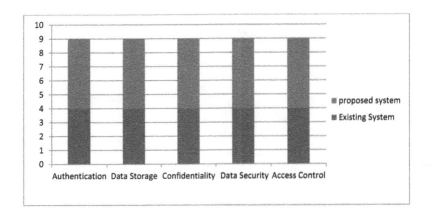

10
9
8
7
6
5
4
3
2
1
0

Authentication Data Storage Confidentiality Data Security Access Control

■ proposed system
■ Existing System

Chart: 3.2 Comparative Charts for Proposed System

- In the existing system, for the cloud computing security has many merits, but still there will be some lack of mechanism to support the trusted computing in cloud computing system. The trusted root in cloud computing environment has not been defined clearly. The creation of protection is not secure enough for cloud computing environments. And there is also lack of mechanism to make data more secure. In the existing system, *Authentication, confidentiality and integrity* were not provided in a better way by using Cryptographic technique as a major factor.

- Trusted Computing Technology is being developed to the network computing, especially the distributed systems environment. The cloud computing is a promising distributed system model and will act as an important role in the e-business or research environments. By providing *Authentication, confidentiality, Data Security, Data Storage and integrity* in a secure Manner "A trusted computing with cryptographic technique" model is established.

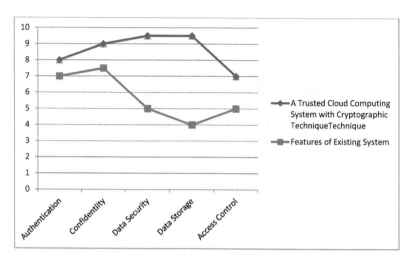

Graph 3.1: A Trusted Cloud Computing with Cryptographic Technique Graphical Representation

3.2 Results

In this chapter our main aim is to evaluate the performance of *"A trusted computing with Cryptographic Technique"* the system can be used to improve security concerns in cloud computing system, using Authentication, confidentiality, Data Storage and integrity as security parameters using Cryptographic technique as major concern. The main issue with the "Cloud" is linked to the responsiveness of information. In a cloud, each of us is completely right to be concerned about the confidentiality, availability and integrity of the information. Tomorrow's world will be based on information. But the future is becoming gradually more doubtful. Information is a critical resource that requires severe controls and protection.

- On using this cryptographic technique (symmetric key encryption) as a major concern the complete module is developed to integrate into trusted computing technology.
- The storage of Cloud customer data will be secure and authentic

24

- Administrator cannot access the cloud customer data without customer's symmetric key
- All cloud files are available in the cloud storage system, on requesting to admin, can provide the concern USER ID of the file. To access the data with symmetric key.
- In the existing cloud computing security system there will be only one way security features has been implemented, taking unique master key as a major constrain.
- In the proposed cloud computing security system, there will be two way security features has been developed taking existing system in to consideration with having additional features of Cryptographic technique (symmetric key).

Trusted platform Support Service TSS components are the major parts of the TCP enabled cloud computing. In our design, TSS should be a bridge between the up-application and the low-hardware. Trusted platform Support Service (TSS) includes two layers, the TSS service provider (TSP) and TSS core services (TCS). The applications call the function of TSP. TSP provides some basic security function modules. These basic modules send calls to TCS. Then TSS converts these calls to according TPM instructions. Since TPM is hardware, the TCG Device Driver Library (TDDL) is necessary. TDDL convert the calls from TCS to the TPM orders. After the TPM process the order, it will return the results up forward. Each layer gets results from low layer and coverts them to responding results that the up layer needs. The main issue with the "Cloud" is linked to the responsiveness of information. In a cloud, each of us is completely right to be concerned about the confidentiality and the availability of the information. Tomorrow's world will be based on information. But the future is becoming gradually more doubtful. Information is a critical resource that requires severe controls and protection.

Trusted Computing technology creates a safer environment in cloud computing. It provides Safer Remote Access through a Combination of mechanism and User Authentication. Trusted computing Protects against data leakage by confirmation of platform integrity prior to encryption and decryption. The Hardware Protection for Encryption and Authentication Key is used by Data (Files) and Communications (Email, Network Access). The Hardware Protection for individually Identifiable Information such as User Ids and Passwords. Lowest Cost Hardware Security

Solution: No Token to Distribute or Lose, No Peripheral to Buy or Plug In, No Limit to Number of Keys, Files or IDs Protected.

- Trusted Computing Protect Business Critical Data and Systems.
- Secure Authentication and Strong Protection of User IDs.
- Establish Strong Machine Identity and Integrity.
- Ensure Regulatory Compliance with Hardware-Based Security.
- Trusted Computing Reduce the Total Cost of Ownership through "Built In" Protection.

Symmetric key Encryption (private key generated)

"A Trusted Cloud Computing with Cryptographic Technique" provides symmetric key encryption and private key will be generated at every aspect of the data upload and download. Same key should be used to encrypt the data and to decrypt the data. On integrating this kind of technology to the trusted computing platform the data security in cloud and data transferred from the cloud system will be in safe and secure way.

Chapter – IV

Summary and Conclusion

4.1 Summary

We can say that the integration of trusted computing technology in to cloud computing system can be used to improve the security concerns of the cloud computing environment. The system titled *""A Trusted Cloud Computing with Cryptographic Technique" is* a long term project; this is designed to provide the security in cloud computing environment by integrating the trusted computing technology using cryptographic technique as a platform into cloud computing system. The proposed modules are -- Authentication, Access control, Data security, Mechanism to trace user behavior in the cloud. Due to implementation this system the security will established in cloud computing environment. We will make the actual design more practical and operational in the imminent. In future, we would also like to study over the impact of more security in this proposed method.

4.2 Conclusion

One of the biggest security issues with the cloud computing model is the sharing of resources.. Cloud service providers need to inform their customers on the level of security that they provide on their cloud. In this paper, we first discussed various models of cloud computing, security issues and research challenges in cloud computing. Data security is major issue for Cloud Computing. Here we proposed all the security issues of cloud computing. We believe that due to the complexity of the cloud, it will be difficult to achieve end-to-end security.

We have analyzed the trusted computing in the cloud computing environment and the function of trusted computing platform in the cloud computing. The advantages of our proposed approach are to extend the trusted computing technology into the cloud computing environment to achieve the trusted computing requirements for the cloud computing and then fulfill the trusted cloud computing. Trusted computing platform is used to provide cloud computing system some important security functions, such as Authentication communication security and data protection.

Now we are developing a model system of trusted cloud computing, which is based on the trusted computing platform and can provide flexible secure services for users.

4.3 Further Scope

The advantages of our planned approach are extending the trusted computing technology to accomplish its requirements for the cloud computing and then fulfill the trusted cloud computing. To integrate these hardware modules with cloud computing system is a difficult work and need more unfathomable study. We develop a model system of trusted cloud computing, which is based on the trusted computing platform. It can provide stretchy security services for users. The Trusted Computing Platform provides cloud computing a sheltered base for achieve trusted computing. We will make the actual design more practical and operational in the imminent. In future, we would also like to study over the impact of more security in this proposed method.

REFERENCES

[1]   Amazon EC2 Crosses the Atlantic. http://aws.amazon.com/about-aws/whats-new/2008/12/10/amazon-ec2-crosses-the-atlantic/

[2]   Amazon S3 Availability Event: July 20, 2008. http://status.aws.amazon.com/s3-20080720.html.

[3]   Amazon's terms of use. http://aws.amazon.com/agreement.

[4]   An Information-Centric Approach to Information Security. http://virtualization.sys-con.com/node/171199.

[5]   AOL apologizes for release of user search data. http://news.cnet.com/2100-1030_3-6102793.html.

[6]   Armbrust, M., Fox, A., Griffith, R. et al. Above the Clouds: A Berkeley View of Cloud Computing. UCB/EECS-2009-28, EECS Department, University of California, Berkeley, 2009.

[7]   Ateniese, G., Burns, R., Curtmola, R., Herring, J., Kissner, L., Z., Peterson, and Song, D. Provable Data Possession at Untrusted Stores. In CCS. 2007.

[8]   Balachandra Reddy Kandukuri, Ramacrishna PaturiV, Atanu Rakshi, "Cloud Security I ssues",IEEE International Conference on Services Computing, pages(s):517-520, 2009.

[9]   Blue Cloud. http://www-03.ibm.com/press/us/en/pressrelease/26642.wss.

[10]   Boneh, B., Di Crescenzo, G., Ostrovsky, R., and Persiano, G. Public Key Encryption

[11]   Boneh, D and Waters, B. Conjunctive, Subset, and Range Queries on Encrypted Data. In The Fourth Theory of Cryptography Conference (TCC 2007), 2007.

[12]   Chor, B., Kushilevitz, E., Goldreich, O., and Sudan, M. Private Information Retrieval. J. ACM, 45, 6 (1998), 965-981.

[13]   CLOIDIFIN. http://community.zdnet.co.uk/blog/0,1000000567,2000625196b,00.htm?new_comment.

[14]   Cloud Bursts as Coghead Calls It Quits. http://blogs.zdnet.com/collaboration/?p=349.

[15]   Cloud computing: Don't get caught without an exit strategy. http://www.computerworld.com/action/article.do?command=viewArticleBasic&articleId=9128665&source=NLT_AM.

[16]   CloudComputing:http://en.wikipedia.org/wiki/Cloud computing, Accessed: 28/07/2011.

[17]   Cloud Computing, http://www.techno-pulse.com/ Cloud Computing for Beginners,
         Accessed: 28/07/2011.

[18]   Cloud Security Alliance: Security Guidance Critical Areas of Focus in Cloud Computing,
         http://www.cloudsecurityalliance.org/guidance/csaguide.pdf. April 2009.

[19]   Disaster-Proofing The Cloud. http://www.forbes.com/2008/11/24/cio-cloud-disaster-tech-cio-
         cx_dw_1125cloud.html.

[20]   Don't cloud your vision. http://www.ft.com/cms/s/0/303680a6-bf51-11dd-ae63-
         0000779fd18c.html?nclick_check=1.

[21]   EMC, Information-Centric Security.
         http://www.idc.pt/resources/PPTs/2007/IT&Internet_Security/12.EMC.pdf.

[22]   Frank E. Gillett, "Future View: The new technology ecosystems of cloud, cloud services
         and cloud computing" Forrester Report, August 2008.

[23]   Glen Bruce, Rob Dempsey, "Security in Distributed Computing", Published by Prentice
         Hall, Copyright Hewlett-Packard Company, 1997.

[24]   Glen Bruce, Rob Dempsey, "Security in Distributed Computing", Published by Prentice
         Hall, Copyright Hewlett-Packard Company, 1997.

[25]   ISO/IEC. Information technology-Open Systems Interconnection- Evaluation criteria for
         information tech-nology, Standard ISO/IEC 15408.1999.

[26]   Jason Reid Juan M. González Nieto Ed Dawson, "Privacy and Trusted Computing",
         Proceedings of the 14th International Workshop on Database and Expert Systems
         Applications, IEEE, 2003.

[27]   Jason Reid Juan M. González Nieto Ed Dawson, "Privacy and Trusted Computing",
         Proceedings of the 14th International Workshop on Database and Expert Systems
         Applications, IEEE, 2003.

[28]   Proceedings of the18th Annual IEEE Symposium on Logic in Computer Science
         (LICS'03), 2003

[29]   Peter Wayner, "Cloud versus cloud – A guided tour of Amazon, Google, AppNexus and
         GoGrid", InfoWorld, July 21, 2008.

[30]   Peter Wayner, "Cloud versus cloud – A guided tour of Amazon,Google, AppNexus and
         GoGrid", InfoWorld, July 21, 2008

www.ingramcontent.com/pod-product-compliance
Lightning Source LLC
La Vergne TN
LVHW042307060326
832902LV00009B/1320